BREATHTAKING!

Discover and Release Your Greatness

By Donna K Woolam

2014 Edition

The information contained within this book is the opinion of the Author only and is not meant to diagnose, treat nor endorse any particular treatment for mental health issues. The Author is not a doctor nor clinician.

Comments, Questions or Suggestions?
All feedback welcomed at
Donna@DonnaWoolam.com

Dedication

For my Richard who has always believed in me.

For my Mother who still doesn't believe she is wonderful.

For my Sister Glynda who makes me better every day.

As We Begin

Life is tricky for a woman. I guess it's probably tricky for men too, but that isn't the focus today.

My hope is that within these pages you'll find something, somewhere, from someone that will help you believe the **TRUTH** about who you are in this world. **YOU are BREATHTAKING.**

You may question why I would say that since we probably haven't even met. Experience has shown me that most women don't feel <u>BREATHTAKING</u> or WONDERFUL. We WANT to be Wonderful; to have a meaningful life and to believe that our being alive makes a difference. But let's get real, most of the time we're just moving from one task to another, one activity to another, one load of laundry to another, and by the end of the day we wonder if we have accomplished anything of meaning or lasting value.

In the movie, *I Don't Know How She Does It*, the main character played by Sarah Jessica Parker, ends every evening in bed with a list going through her head. The list includes the things she didn't get done, the things she didn't do well and the things she has to do tomorrow. By the end of the movie, for her at least, there is some resolution to her soul-numbing quest for excellence in all the areas of her life. I don't know about you but I don't have any script-writers running around my house to make sure everything falls well within the 90 minute guidelines of a movie.

What you're about to read, and experience (I hope), is a concept that is transforming a lot of women that I know. I've experienced it personally and I've witnessed it over and over again. It is simply a concept of women helping women to become their very best self. And it is done not by telling a woman how to do the laundry in between soccer games, but by helping a woman discover the great gifts that lay within her, to own them and then, to release them.

I believe that the greatest Source of Transformation is found within the Light of a Loving God. If you want to categorize me spiritually, I'm a Christian. I'm a Radical Grace Christian if you want to hem it in a bit more. For me, that simply means I believe that the literal Life, Death and Resurrection of Jesus Christ changed everything; and, that when you really believe that every judgment of God (aka Wrath of God) was paid for by the Finished Work of Jesus on the Cross, all that is left to do is live out life through the Completed Work of Reconciliation. Knowing this I can live totally free to express all that God created me to be.

Ephesians 2:10 - For we are God's masterpiece. He has created us anew in Christ Jesus, so we can do the good things he planned for us long ago. (NLT)

This writing is not meant to be about Christian philosophy nor is it a treatise on how to be a better Christian. I thought it fair to set out from the beginning where my foundations rest. Does that mean we can't participate together if we don't believe everything the same way? I certainly hope it doesn't, or I've totally missed being able to communicate the heart of what this is meant to be and become.

My desire is that this will feel like a conversation between friends; two people sitting down over a cup of coffee or a fine glass of wine. We'll talk about how the day went, what we witnessed, how we wish we could change some things, and discover how together we can do something to fix what is challenging our lives. I hope you can hear my heart and my voice, and that you'll feel like it's my hand reaching out to yours to support you to release the **Breathtaking, Wonderful Woman** that you already are.

Table of Contents

Contents

Under Pressure!

Darling Woman reading this, understand that you are worthy and valuable simply because you are alive in this world! My life's calling is helping women discover the intrinsic worth that is birthed within each and every one of us.

Our world strives to convince us that we are anything BUT incredible! Is it any surprise that we spend hours in front of the mirror wondering if our hair is just right, or our makeup the right kind, or our clothes fashionable enough? Hey, you and I both know that most of us don't dress for the men in the room; we dress for the women, because we know that somebody will say something! Does anyone else brighten up when someone says, 'I love your dress,' or 'your hair is so cute!'

The media edits photos of women to make the average woman feel fat, unattractive and worthless in an effort to sell the next hottest product. I heard Cheryl Tiegs say on a talk show, *"I wish I looked like my picture on that magazine cover."* Throughout many parts of the world, women are still considered property. A so-called prettier woman is worth more than an 'average' woman; a certain type of woman is called a trophy wife. Who defines pretty anyway? "Pretty" is a transitory term that is defined by what we're told by the media and the fashion of the day. Marilyn Monroe or Twiggy? Jennifer Aniston or Katy Perry? Jennifer Lopez or Pink? Does anyone else get tired of the obvious difference made between older men in the media and older women? An older, grayer man is 'sexy' while an older, grayer woman is just old.

We can't just blame THEM (whoever they are.) We are victims of not just the pressures 'the world' puts on us, but the pressures we as women put upon one another and we, as individuals, put upon ourselves. The pressure to be a certain size, have a certain hair color, be a certain race, be a certain age or have a certain personality all conspire to make women consider our outward appearance as the measuring stick of whether or not we are valuable. And for most of us, we place our worth and value at a very low level. Because of this we are plagued with eating disorders, sexual dysfunction, abusive relationships and squandered talents.

And it doesn't seem to really matter what we do because it just isn't the right thing! Why is it that a powerful woman is considered aggressive or a *itch or that a woman who wants to build a career is neglectful of her family? Then again, there is the woman who chooses to be a stay at home wife and mother who is considered 'lazy' or refuses to "take advantage' of all of her opportunities. And the woman who tries to 'do it all' and 'be it all' - well she's just CRAZY! And these aren't the views of men; they are the words of women to women about women!

And hey, I remember walking down the street with a female friend of mine during my high school days.

We had just received our school annuals and she told me she wouldn't let girls sign hers because 'girls are so mean.' Pretty is as pretty does.

When I was in my mid-30's I worked for a staffing agency. The founder and owner was a 'mature' woman (read over 45.) The sales reps she chose for that company were trim, blonde and under 35. Why? Because they could more easily get into an office to see the human resource managers of our clients and potential clients. Let's make it clear, our business was to support the companies, not the part time or potential full time employees we sent for jobs. I worked as a liaison between our employees and client companies. When calls came in for job openings for front office positions, I was told repeatedly by the owner of our company that I should only send young, attractive girls or we'd lose the contract. Sadly it didn't matter how qualified she was (or wasn't) for the job. I remember one last minute request on a holiday weekend. No one wanted to work and the only woman I could send out was an older (read older than 35), heavier (probably 150), highly qualified candidate. The owner of the client company called and told us 'we had better not send him any more clowns' to do the job. Is it illegal? Of course! Is it still done? You betcha! Forget about equal rights for women working alongside men. What about equal rights for women working alongside women!

Ok, so, I know that this sounds like I'm beating up on the pretty girls. Honestly, I'm not! I know a lot of stunningly beautiful women who feel just as worn and weary from all of these things as anyone else. Maybe even more so because she wonders if the only thing anyone ever notices is her looks. We still live in a society where a woman's intellect is not as important as her appearance. SHAME ON US! As Forrest Gump said, 'stupid is as stupid does.'

It can change. We were created by God to walk confidently and boldly in this world exhibiting all of His Grace and Power through the gifts we have been given. We can be our own best hero by discovering for ourselves what our hopes and dreams are and begin working toward them. We can bring about change by advocating for one another in everyday life. We can create change for our daughters and granddaughters by teaching them about the truth of their worth.

By working together, we can bring out the greatness that is in each of us. I'm not talking about radical feminism. I'm talking about being the woman you were created to be without shying away from all the intricacies that involves. We are strong and tender. We are wise and silly. We are smart and fragile. We are beautiful in all of the ways we are - tall, short, petite, round, thin, color upon color, and age upon age.

> *"Above all, be the heroine of your life, not the victim."*
> *Nora Ephron*

A Few Scary Statistics

90% of all women want to change at least one aspect of their physical appearance.

81% of 10 year old girls are afraid of being fat.

Women are routinely degraded in everything from pop culture to casual conversation.

A girl is bullied every 7 minutes in the school yard, playground, stairwell, classroom or bathroom.

Every 15 seconds a woman is battered.

57% of rock music videos portray women as a sex object, a victim, as unintelligent, or in a condescending way.

57% of women are targeted for workplace bullying.

47% of students have been hazed prior to coming to college.

One in three girls who have been in a serious relationship say they've been concerned about being physically hurt by their partner.

Women are devalued in the workplace, making only 76% of their male peers' salaries.

Girls are more likely than boys to be victims of cyber bullying.

One in four college-age women have an eating disorder.

Suicide is the 3rd leading cause of death among adolescents and teenagers. Teen girls are more likely to attempt suicide.

Women make up nearly 51% of the population, but hold just 16% of the seats in Congress.

Three-fourths of girls with low self-esteem engage in negative activities, such as disordered eating, bullying, smoking or drinking.

Only 2% of women think they are beautiful.

One in three girls between the ages of 16 and 18 say sex is expected for people their age if they're in a relationship.

Statistics from: www.confidencecoalition.org

You are Breathtaking!

Breathtaking: 1) making one out of breath; 2) a: exciting, thrilling; b: very great; astonishing

Is this how you see yourself? Do you know in the very core of your being that YOU are Exciting? Thrilling? Very Great? Astonishing?

It's a dizzying experience when you are 'in your space' being who you are created to be. It seems like everything is easier and more meaningful and suddenly your whole world makes sense.

I wish I could see your eyes right now! I'd love to be looking into your face to tell you that you are valuable! You are incredible! You are BREATHTAKING and worth more than you know! More often than not, what I've seen when I tell a woman such a thing is a look of disbelief. More like, "Yeah. Right," instead of "YOU'RE RIGHT!"

We are extraordinary created beings. Unfortunately most of us don't experience that knowledge on a day to day basis. Even though we are created with an incredible capacity to organize systems, maintain order, creatively launch businesses, sustain life within ourselves, nurture generations, and support others to greatness we often feel 'less than' or that we are failing in the things that are most important to us. (These, by the way, are just a few of the things the Proverbs 31 woman is praised for being, so it isn't just my opinion, it is the Bible.)

The nature of most women is to carry the responsibility of a successful home on her shoulders. Even if she does have the support of a husband, when something goes wrong, the woman typically, albeit subconsciously, takes the blame. Unfortunately, society also blames us.

A lot of you make the choice to work at home full time. Caring for the family and household is your primary occupation. (NEVER tell this woman she doesn't WORK!)

Many of you hold a job away from home (sometimes more than one) and are still the primary organizer for the household. Even in our modern society it is still primarily 'the woman's job' to take care of the family needs and household necessities - cooking, cleaning, laundry, shopping, homework, sports events, social events and extracurricular activities. Okay I get it, for some of you reading this it sounds archaic, but in my experience most 2-parent households are still run this way.

Without skipping a beat, we also have the all-important work of building strong relationships with our children and our husbands; insert here: bed time stories, enhanced learning opportunities and events, meals around the table, date night, and romantic getaways. More and more of the women I know also find themselves in the role of caregiver for parents and/or in-laws. This adds an entirely different set of responsibilities; travel to and from doctors' appointments, helping to find and maintain suitable living arrangements, hiring and overseeing home care, all while maintaining an attitude of a child and not a boss. *(Just TRY and boss my mom!)*

If you're a single woman, you are carrying all the weight of earning an income to supply the needs of a financial reality where the income you earn may not even meet the needs of basic existence. Many times you have 'extra' family responsibilities simply because 'you're single.' It is assumed you have more time and energy to take care of things that others don't or won't.

Can I get a standing ovation for all of the single mothers? You can find yourself with an intense struggle to keep everything together as both mom and dad. Most likely there is little emotional support for you at home. Without an extended network of people for support, the simple state of being a single parent can become overwhelming.

In the midst of these responsibilities, we women are busy. We are busy being good friends; caring for others, organizing fundraisers for our heartfelt causes and a multitude of other activities that keep us BUSY. "Exhausted" threatens to become an everyday state of being. Even thinking about doing 'something for ourselves' just adds more stress.

I believe that in today's world we women need one another more than ever before. Our social media driven world gives us the appearance of connection but really separates us. There are fewer 'girl's nights out' because we can just "check-in" through

Facebook, Pinterest or Twitter. It used to be that women were surrounded by mentors to show them how to navigate the waters of life. We are made for relationship and community and because we aren't truly connecting, we are struggling.

You may not feel like you are BREATHTAKING, but I bet reading over this most of us feel OUT OF BREATH!

It's so important for you to get this point right here and right now: being WONDERFUL and BREATHTAKING isn't a matter of all you DO! It's all you ARE in the doing. Out of the very essence of your being, usually without any formal training, you bring forth organizational skills, educational talents, schedule mastery, compassionate works of grace for the broken and struggling, and many more instinctive qualities. And, you do all of these things without thinking because THAT is who you are at your core!

What Happened to That Little Girl?

Or, Who Am I and Why Should You Care?

When I was a little girl I was full of joy. I was a singer and a talker. I do remember that I spent a lot of time in the first and second grades in the hall for 'talking too much.' Most of my report cards carried a check for excessive talking.

I was a spinner. You know, the kind of little girl who spins so her dress will fly out in a circle of lace. I danced and sang in my room. I loved dramatic, old movies from the 30's and 40's! **Stage Door** was my absolute favorite movie - all of those women living out their dreams in the Big City. Some were wildly successful, some changed their dream and some slipped away in despair. Still today I can hear
Katherine Hepburn saying, *"The calla lilies are in bloom again. Such a strange flower; I carried them at my wedding and today I carry them in memory of something that has died."*

Sometime around the age of 8 or 9 the little girl that was me began to fade away. I know that honesty and vulnerability here is important, but it feels tricky. I bet you feel that way too, when you are trying to find the root reasons for feeling and playing smaller than you know you could. Somehow, all the joy and singing and dancing ran out of my life. How could that happen? Where did I go?

My mom was often ill. She was in the hospital for different reasons. What I remember most is that she was sad. A lot. I came to understand that depression was her constant companion.

When my mom was in the hospital family took care of me; grandparents, aunts, uncles, cousins, my dad, my brothers, and my sisters-in-law. All of them loved me and were wonderful. The thing is, what I wanted was my mom. I felt so separated from her and that somehow I was a burden to her. My imagination ran rampant. Once I remember sitting on the bed crying, believing it was my fault that she was going away. I thought I was adopted and went on a hunt for the adoption papers. I remember writing notes to my mom and leaving them on her pillow saying things like, 'I need to talk to you,' because I felt like I was an imposition. I never felt like I could just be me with her, and that when I was, it somehow wasn't enough. I felt like my love, my achievements, even my accomplishments were always just shy of the mark that I needed to attain in order to be acceptable. Funny thing is that's how she felt. Her pain became the garment I wore for years.

I have a picture from the fifth grade. The little 10 year old girl in that picture has dark circles and bags under her forlorn green eyes. Her longish, blond hair is disheveled. The collar on her delicate, green dress is askew. She is so sad and has a look of longing; longing for someone to really SEE her. My eldest brother says that it makes him sad when he sees that picture and that he didn't realize what kind of shape I was in at that time. I wasn't abused nor neglected - just lonely. Sadness surrounded our home and I guess it entered my heart.

As I've learned more about my Mom's life I've come to understand her better. She was a child of the Depression Era. They were dirt farmers in Oklahoma and Texas and there was little money and few resources. Living with my Granddad was pretty hard. My Grandma had heart problems so my Mom grew up early in order to help take care of the family. During her tender years, Mom witnessed the death of a baby brother. Mom always believed that her siblings were more loved than she, that they were more beautiful/handsome, and so ultimately, more important.

She was raised as a woman in an age when boys were king, so her dreams were considered silly. Education was critically important to her, but she didn't get to pursue a college degree. Mom didn't let it stop her, though. She became self-educated and was a voracious reader. (Books, magazines and the daily newspaper still surround her chair every day!) I remember in the 1970's she took a job at a local hospital in the financial department. She had to learn computer skills. It was a big deal back then and she worked very hard to learn the systems. Because she wanted to be educated, eloquent and informed, many of her extended family ridiculed her and thought she was a snob. Mom had so many dreams and hopes, one of which was to be a writer. Only a few of her dreams have come to pass and I believe that has been an integral part of her years of sadness and depression.

I don't mean to make it sound like everything was bad. Mom held a surprise birthday party for me when I was 8. I remember playing 'Poor Kitty' and having all my friends around me. I can still see her face working to make me laugh. She made sure that I had violin lessons and an incredibly beautiful violin. Somehow, somewhere she found the money to send me to music camp for a couple of summers, she sat outside for hours while I took advantage of advanced music classes. She fought for me to have the things I wanted when she could. I wish I had appreciated it more.

Mom wanted more for all of us. Somehow, we interpreted that to mean she wasn't proud of us. How strange when I think back on it now. When it was in her power, she always made sure we had the resources to take advantage of learning opportunities. She taught us to stand up tall, to speak correctly, the importance of making a good first impression. She wanted us to crave knowledge and be lifelong learners. She and my dad worked hard to provide financially for us and we had a pretty good life. But because I was raised by a woman who wanted 'more', I became a woman who thought that 'more' meant better.

What is incredible to me about my Mom's story is that it could be the story of any woman today. We just haven't changed that much even with all of our modern conveniences and support systems. Faced with hardship, today's woman isn't able to follow her dreams. It whittles away at her confidence; feelings of inadequacy cause her to make choices that aren't the best for her; she sacrifices who she is intrinsically, instead of giving the people she cares about her best self. Ah, there she is. My Mom is today's woman living inside an 87-year old woman.

(Thankfully I can report that my mom and I have a much better relationship now. She is in her late 80's at the time of this writing. We've worked for years to heal and create a relationship based on honesty. It hasn't always been easy but it has definitely been worth it. You see, I didn't want to lose her - or for her to lose me - and to live out life with regret. As my life has become more complicated by the sickness of my husband, I've begun to appreciate her journey even more.)

I wanted to be FREE! Most teenagers do! I met my Richard when I was 17 years old. He was 24 and had striking blue eyes; long, sun-bleached brown hair and a mustache. He came from California, drove a sweet little red Datsun pickup and carried his tri- color Australian Shepherd, Lady Bear, in the back. I was SMITTEN! He didn't know anything about me or my past, so I could be anyone I wanted. I decided to be myself. Oddly, it was enough. To be transparently honest, I did make some compromises to impress him. But mostly I chose the real me over the imaginary me. For years I lived in blissful unawareness of what was lacking. I was happy to be me. When we had our boys, I began to yearn again for those things that would make us 'better'; better home, better clothes, better toys.

Now, there's nothing wrong with that desire! But when it makes you consider that *you* are less because you *have* less, there is an issue. Sacrifice for your family is honorable and common and SHOULD happen. I'm not here to say it should be all-about-what-you-want-and-who-cares-what-happens-to-the-family. Please remember that my goal here is to help us not have to sacrifice our uniqueness in the process. My goal is to try and find a way to help us all be the BEST VERSION of ourselves that is possible. The most complete, the most fulfilled, the most giving, the most serving, and the most loving; without becoming broken and hollow in the pouring out.

Oh! Women!

For the past 20+ years, I've been able to work with women in all kinds of situations; from ministry-based church activities to business expos, seminars and one-on-one business coaching strategy sessions.

Early in my business life I discovered the concepts of Legacy and Shepherd Leadership principles. Those principles have not only helped me learn how to teach, but also how to empower a woman and help her pass that empowerment along to others.

I've met women from all walks of life; ministry leaders, stay-at-home wives and moms, corporate executives, business owners, across-the-cubicle work sisters, business partners, hostesses of home sales parties, and others who were guests of those hostesses. I have visited homes of women from all kinds of backgrounds; economically, racially, socially, and spiritually. I've met women of all ages. I'm sure that I have personally interacted with several thousands of women over the course of the last 20 years.

Because of my own background, I shouldn't be shocked by what I've learned about women through these interactions. I've come to understand that most women do not really know how incredible they are! Many women experience a very low level of self-worth. What self-worth they do have is dependent upon what they have, how they look, or what their families have done or accomplished. We're good at wearing our 'everything is fine' mask, but when we are alone, or with only very trusted friends, our feelings of failure at measuring up begin to sneak out.

Most of us have a story of someone special and important whom we felt we couldn't please. We have struggled for acceptance in a world that wants to shove us all into the same mold. We are unique, and wonderful, and fabulous, and creative, and magnificent, and *BREAKTAKING;* but we don't accept it! When we do realize how unique we are, we usually use that as a reason to feel like we don't belong, instead of letting it become the wings that cause us to soar.

I believe that women can be anything they want to be; single, married, childless, child-full, work at home, work in the corporate world, or even run the corporate world, that choice is each individual woman's. We as women have a responsibility to support one another in our choices.

I remember one friend in particular. We met at a get-together and eventually became business partners. She was (is) fun to be around but always put herself down. I knew her to be highly skilled and extremely intelligent. She is the epitome of 'good mom'. I could tell that she didn't have a very high self- opinion. Her personal appearance was a bit unkempt, and her general outlook on life was fairly negative. People loved her, but she was a bit on the razor's edge when it came to humor and interaction. She was my friend, and she needed someone to believe in her until she could believe more in herself. I learned that her background was one of constant negativity and feelings of 'less-than'. Over the years of our friendship, I saw her blossom and bloom as the true leader she had always been. As she began to believe in herself, those garments of the past began to fall away. She is now an incredible leader in the working community, in the civic community and in the church world. All of the things that were incredible within her began to come to the forefront once she knew and believed that she was and is, BREATHTAKING. She now passes on a legacy of wholeness to all the women and girls she meets. She inspires me to be a better person. *(Love you girl. You know who you are.)*

How Do We Change Things?

It's all well and good to have an opinion about how life is for a woman, but how do we change anything?

In the following pages, allow me to make a few suggestions as to what we can do that will make a difference.

Step 1: **Look Inward** - Discover who YOU are and what is important to you (your core values.)

In this section, we'll take our time identifying the things that are important to you and why. Using some time-honored tools and techniques, you'll be able to discover how closely you are living to the way you want to live. You'll also begin to understand the things that are most important to you and how to have more of those things in your life, while leaving behind the things that are not as important.

Step 2: **Look Outward** - Define what a MENTOR is and what a mentor does.

Just what is a mentor and what does a mentor do, and why should you think about being one and having one?

The greatest leaders in our society have people speak into their life. All of us have been influenced in one way or another by people around us. This section will help us identify what to look for in a mentor and how to become an intentional mentor for others.

Step 3: **Look Around** - Identify areas where you can use your gifts, callings, talents and core values to become a mentor. Also, identify areas where you could use a mentor to assist you in reaching your life goals.

Having gathered all of the information from Steps 1 and 2, we will begin to examine where we can put the information to use. We'll pull together a sampling of resources to meet with your point of view: from Social Media and the Political realms to the Church and Community Involvement.

Step 4: **Look Forward** - Creating Legacy by interacting with the next generation.

How do we create better experiences for the women who are following us? In this section we'll discuss ways that we can join together and create an environment for wholeness for future generations.

Look Inward

Discover who YOU are and what is important to you
(Your Core Values)

Webster's Dictionary defines **Believe** as: *to accept or regard (something) as true; to accept the truth of what is said by (someone); to have (a specified opinion)*

In this section we're going to talk about a few different kinds of belief.

I Am - What you believe about yourself.

I Believe - What your core beliefs are, with regard to the things that are important to you.

I Want - What you believe is possible for your life.

I See - What you believe about the world around you and how you fit into it.

As you go through the following sections of the "Look Inward" step, you will find some exercises to complete. For the most part, these are gut reaction exercises. That simply means, I want you to answer from your heart - not your head. We want to get to the CORE of your belief systems and thought patterns.

Don't spend a lot of time analyzing or thinking about the right answer; because there isn't one. There is only YOUR answer. This is a time of self-discovery. Take advantage of learning more about yourself so that you can reap the benefit of knowing you!

On your second go around (after you've completed ALL of the exercises in the book), take the tests again more slowly to see if your beliefs have changed.

It's okay if things don't have a complete shift overnight. Hey - we didn't get this way in one day. I'm still on the journey, too.

Some of the exercises will require 45 minutes or so. Most are fairly quick; circle, mark, write a short answer.

Don't be overwhelmed. They aren't difficult - although I hope they are challenging.

These are NOT meant to provide a clinical, psychological analysis, nor a medical diagnosis for any condition or state of mind. I am not a doctor. These are simply tools I have found helpful and I'm sharing them.

Where possible, I'm giving credit where credit is due, to the person or organization that first shared the exercise with me. Some of them have been with me for so long I don't honestly know where they came from. You'll find all of that information in the endnotes if you want to learn more.

You can find extra worksheets for the exercises on my website in the *Breathtaking!* Resources section.

I Am...

In order to LIVE OUT and BE the wonderful woman that you already are, you need to believe it first.

What do you believe about yourself? I'm talking about the "honestly-believe" part when you're all alone, and no one sees you, nor hears you; the innermost thoughts of your innermost being. I know, it's a challenging question. The first time I asked myself this and really thought about it, I cried a lot.

What we **want** to believe about who we are, and what we **actually** believe are, for most women, miles apart.

Faced day-by-day with our own fears and perceived failures, we subconsciously rip away the belief that we are worthy of a life of conscious satisfaction and joy. We judge ourselves against the words of the past, the people we see every day, and the expectations we have for our future.

That's not to say that all areas of our lives are a mess. We may have a pretty healthy self-awareness when it comes to our professional success, but not so great with our personal appearance. Or, maybe we're great in our family relationships, but we know our work life is a mess.

When we tell ourselves that we are too old, too young, too poor, too inexperienced, or too (insert anything,) we limit our ability to believe the best about ourselves. You may have heard the saying that we always compare the WORST of ourselves with the BEST in others (and sometimes visa-versa.) True self-worth will bring about true self-confidence. That is, when we begin to understand our own personal worth and value, we stop degrading others. Instead, a heart of compassion begins to grow within us and when we see someone struggling, our first question isn't "What's wrong with them?" but, "How can I assist them?"

In the next few pages, you're going to take an in-depth look at what you believe about yourself and why. Even though these are meant to be taken somewhat quickly and answered from gut level, expect that you will feel some emotional tugs. It is important to let yourself experience the emotions. They will be a key to the areas that you want to change or enhance. The areas that give you joy will be the places that give you a clue to the areas of strength in your life - the areas where you are able to soar right now (or very soon.) The areas that bring sorrow are the places that are causing you pain and loss. These are the areas that you most likely have received a wound and need some emotional healing and support.

Shall we begin?

Exercise #1

IN THE FIRST COLUMN, simply write down all of the roles you fill in your everyday life: things like daughter, mother, sister, employee, and boss.

IN THE SECOND COLUMN, (a bit trickier here) - write down the GRADE you give yourself for that role; A-D, just like in school. Remember, this is how you FEEL you are doing.

The Roles I Fill	The Grades I Give To Myself

THIS IS ONLY FOR YOU! No one is going to look over your shoulder and no one will know about this except you unless YOU choose to share it with a friend or loved one.

Next, let's look at the reasons why you gave yourself the grades you have.

Exercise #2

Look at each of your Roles and the Grade you gave yourself. Why did you give yourself each grade? If it is high, why did you grade yourself highly; performance, attitude; awards? If it is low, why did you grade yourself poorly?

Jot those down here:

1. In my Role as_____, I gave myself a grade of_____because:

2. In my Role as_____, I gave myself a grade of_____because:

3. In my Role as_____, I
gave myself a grade of_____because:

4. In my Role as_____, I
gave myself a grade of_____because:

5. In my Role as_____, I
gave myself a grade of_____because:

6. In my Role as_____, I
gave myself a grade of_____because:

7. In my Role as_____, I
gave myself a grade of_____because:

8. In my Role as_____, I
gave myself a grade of_____because:

9. In my Role as_____, I
gave myself a grade of_____because:

10. In my Role as_____, I
gave myself a grade of_____because:

Now, let's identify the foundation for why you gave
yourself these grades.

Exercise #3

In this exercise, the goal is to determine whether your grades are based on Perceived Performance (how you see yourself or think others see you) or on Actual Fact.

Perceived performance is often based upon *OPINION* - something along the lines of 'blondes have more fun.' Because we've been told something like this all of our lives, we begin to perceive that it is true. Perceived performance can also be an indication of our *CORE VALUES,* which we'll discuss further in the next chapter.

Actual fact is based upon any *ACTION* that is actually being performed. For instance, a healthy action could be something like an award for performance at your job or school that recognizes your achievement in an area. An unhealthy action could be something that is detrimental to the health, safety, well-being, or create a long-term result for a person or in a situation. These things could fall into the realm of drugs, alcohol, damaging behaviors, etc.

Some examples of this would be:

Negative Perceived Performance: I'm not a good mother because I don't read my child a bedtime story every night.

Positive Perceived Performance: I'm a good mother because I tell my child I love her every day.

Negative Actual Fact: I'm not a good mother because I leave my young child home alone while I go on a date.

Positive Actual Fact: I'm a good mother because I make sure my child has balanced nutrition nearly every day.

Circle answer A or B and then **write a brief reason why** you chose the answer.

1. The grade I gave myself in my role

as _____
is based upon a) perceived performance or, b) actual fact.

2. The grade I gave myself in my role as

_____
is based upon a) perceived performance or, b) actual fact.

3. The grade I gave myself in my role
as _____
is based upon a) perceived performance or, b) actual fact.

4. The grade I gave myself in my role as _____

is based upon a) perceived performance or, b) actua fact.

5. The grade I gave myself in my role as _____

is based upon a) perceived performance or, b) actual fact.

6. The grade I gave myself in my role as _____

is based upon a) perceived performance or, b) actual fact.

7. The grade I gave myself in my role as _____

is based upon a) perceived performance or, b) actual fact.

8. The grade I gave myself in my role as _____
is based upon a) perceived performance or, b) actual fact.

9. The grade I gave myself in my role as _____
is based upon a) perceived performance or, b) actual fact.

10. The grade I gave myself in my role as _____
is based upon a) perceived performance or, b) actual fact.

Tally up your answers. Give your totals here:
Perceived Performance _____
Actual Fact _____

If your answers lean more to Perception, your life is probably being pushed along by how you think you should live; either based on the opinions of others or your core values. If the opinions of others are not matching with your core values, then you probably feel guilty or unfulfilled a lot of the time. If the perceptions are based on your Core Values and you believe you are doing well in those areas, you probably experience a great deal of contentment. If you believe that you are not doing well in those areas, you most likely feel conflicted between roles.

If your answers lean more to Actual Fact you will find yourself in one of two positions. If you believe that your life is on track, you are most likely experiencing a great deal of contentment based on the choices you've made and the actions you've taken. If you believe that your life is not on track, you most likely experience a great deal of guilt because of your actions. You may become defensive when those actions are questioned because you know at your core that you need to change your behaviors.

The great news is that no matter where you find yourself, it's okay!

If you are living out your life based on your Core Values and the Actions you take match up - CONGRATULATIONS! You are in a strong place and probably already assist others to experience the fulfillment that you have on a regular basis. If you don't, you would like to learn how.

If you are not living out your life based on your Core Values, or aren't sure what those Core Values are, we are about to enter into a short journey that will assist you to identify and implement the things that are most important to you at the center of your being.

If you are not happy about the Actions you are currently taking in your life, there is support for you. Self-discovery enables us to be honest with ourselves. If you are behaving in a way that is damaging to you or others, you can change. There are steps you can take that will bring you to victory.

I Believe...

In this chapter, we are going to take a look at Core Values and Self Talk.

Core Values are those things that are the most important aspect of who we are at the very depth of our being. They are formed by life experiences, our spiritual backgrounds, and the path that we personally want to take in order to achieve our version of success.

In the first section, you will take a short journey toward learning what your Core Values are. This will by no means be an extensive study. There are some incredible resources available both on line and in print. You can find resources geared specifically to your work environment, and others for your personal life exploration.

In the second section, we will discuss Self-Talk and its impact on your everyday life.

Core Values

Some call them PASSIONS. Some call them CORE VALUES. Ultimately, they are the same. They are the ideals that define us as an individual human being.

When we are living according to our core values, we experience life in a deeper way. When our life feels shallow and meaningless, it is often because we are neglecting our core values.

Core Values can show up in conversation. Statements such as, "I don't believe in lying to get my way." or, "We should recycle at every opportunity in order to save our planet."

Core Values can show up in the causes you support. They can make themselves known in the schools and churches you choose.

Core Values help us to live an authentic life. Authenticity breeds confidence, which breeds success. Living outside of the beliefs that are most important to us causes stress, frustration and a feeling that we are not 'being real.'

You probably have a fairly good idea about most of your core values, but just for fun, let's have some more quick exercises to help you define them even further.

Defining Your Core Values

Knowing your Core Values helps you define the activities, jobs, and roles that are most important to you. When you know your values, it helps you make better decisions about where to put your time and effort.

You'll refer back to them over and over again as you make decisions about 'what to do next.'

For example, if FREEDOM is one of your Core Values and FAMILY is one of your Core Values, you probably won't want to take a job that gives you a lot of freedom but takes you away from your family for weeks at a time. However, if the job allows you to work independently AND have your family near to you, it might be something to look into further.

On the following list, circle or highlight 20 of the values that resonate the most with you. It's important to understand there are no 'right' nor 'wrong' answers. This list is just a beginning. [i]

Acceptance	Fast Pace	Power
Achievement	Financial Rewards	Privacy
Adventure	Focus	Productivity
Altruism	Freedom	Promotion Prospects
Ambition	Friendship	Reaching Potential
Appreciation	Fun	Recognition
Authenticity	Happiness	Respect
Authority	Harmony	Responsibility
Autonomy	Health	Results
Balance	Helping Others	Risk Taking
Beauty	Honesty	Romance
Belonging	Humor	Routine
Challenge	Imagination	Security
Choice	Independence	Self-Expression
Collaboration	Influence	Service
Commitment	Intellect	Sharing
Community	Intuition	Solitude
Compassion	Justice	Spirituality
Competition	Kindness	Status
Connection	Leadership	Success
Contribution	Learning	Teaching
Creativity	Love	Team Work

Equality	Loyalty	Tolerance
Excellence	Making a Difference	Tradition
Excitement	Nature	Travel
Expertise	Nurturing	Trust
Fairness	Order	Variety
Faith	Passion	Winning
Fame	Peace	Wisdom
Family	Personal Growth	Zest for Life

Narrow the 20 down to the 10 most important and write them here:

1.

2.

3.

4.

5.

6.

7.

8.

9.

10.

Narrow those 10 down to the 5 most important and write them here:

1.

2.

3.

4.

5.

Now, decide the order of importance. List them in order of HIGHEST to LOWEST importance.

1.

2.

3.

4.

5.

Take some time to write about each of the values and what it means to you. For instance, the word *FREEDOM*. What does that word mean to you? How does it appear in your life and when? You'll want to do this on a separate sheet of paper, or on one of the blank pages at the back of the book.

Are you surprised at the list you created? Did you know that each of these things was the most important to you?

Some of our Core Values may shift a bit throughout life due to new beliefs and perceptions. This is a test to take from time to time, just to make sure you are on track and being your authentic self.

Science tells us that humans have 12,000 to 60,000 thoughts per day. Of those, 70% to 80% are NEGATIVE! Now, all those negative thoughts may not be about you personally, but a good portion of them are. You know the ones: "I can't believe I said that." "I can't believe I ate that." "I can't believe how (insert anything here) this makes me look." "Oh! My hair!"

That means that of the 50,000 thoughts you'll have had by the time you go to sleep tonight, up to 40,000 of them were negative! That's pretty horrible, wouldn't you agree. Even if only a small fraction of them are directed to yourself, is it any wonder that you, along with most women, don't think of yourselves as BREATHTAKING and WONDERFUL?

Looking back to the "I Am" exercises, you can see that how we see ourselves in our Life Roles and how those balance/counter-balance with our Core Values can determine how we think about ourselves and thus, how we talk to ourselves. For our purposes here, Self-talk is defined as the conversation you have with yourself, about yourself.

Like Core Values, Self-Talk is a big topic. You can find some terrific resources if you want to investigate further. This book touches just the top of the subject in order to give you a frame of reference.

Positive, empowering, energizing self-talk takes discipline. It is totally rearranging the way you communicate with yourself. My Grandma Bunch used to say, "If you can't say anything nice, don't say anything at all." Now she meant that about how I should treat other people, but the same holds true to our conversations with ourselves. We often say things to ourselves that we would never allow another human being to say to us!

The Bible tells us in Proverbs 23:7, *"As a man thinks in his heart, so is he"* and in Luke 6:45, *"out of the abundance of the heart, the mouth speaks."*

The things we think and say will manifest themselves in our lives.

I remember a time in my life when everything felt chaotic. All I kept saying, to myself and to everyone who would listen is, "My life is so out of control. Everything is a mess. I can't seem to focus." Guess what! My life was an out of control, unfocused, chaotic mess! When I realized what I was saying, I began to say different things and life changed. I began to say, "My life is becoming more and more controlled every day. I'm able to focus on what I need to achieve. My life is balanced and settled." It changed everything. Not only did my perceptions change, but my actions changed to be in alignment with those thoughts and perceptions.

You break the habits in much the same way a smoker stops smoking; you substitute one set of behaviors with another.

Your next exercises are based on self-observation. Over the next days, pay attention to the words you THINK about yourself and the words you SAY about your life.

It probably won't take more than an hour or two to realize that what you are THINKING and SAYING do not line up with what you WANT in your life.

Exercise #1

As you hear, whether in your mind or out of your mouth, yourself saying things that do not line up with what you want in your life, begin to write them down on 3x5 index cards. Keep a few handy with you at all times. Depending on your personality, you might want to get a variety of colors. You can use a different color for each of the different roles you fill in your life: pink for personal, green for work, etc.

Exercise #2

After you've observed your thought life for a bit, the next exercise is to create a statement that helps you change the thought.

For example, from: "I'll never have a job I like." to "I will find a job that I enjoy." Or, "I hate the way I look in these pants." To "When I shop for clothes I find the ones that make me feel incredible."

Here's what happens. You begin to change your perspective. Some would say, 'the universe' lines up to give you what you expect. This is what I know from my own experience; I worked for a company that had a particular type of car as an incentive. In the city where I lived, I don't remember ever seeing those cars, but as soon as it was announced that I could earn one of that type of car, I saw them everywhere! You see what you expect to see.

Now, do I believe that supernatural power exists? YES! Do I believe that supernatural power works on our behalf? YES! But my personal belief is that it takes more than having a 'good feeling' about something. That's just me. You may think a different way - that's OK. The important thing is that we CHANGE our negative thought and speech patterns to positive thought and speech patterns.

Exercise #3

PRACTICE, PRACTICE, PRACTICE! Every single Day be a drill sergeant over your words and thoughts. Make it your aim to bring them into alignment with your Core Values.

As your Self-Talk changes, you WILL begin to see changes in your life.

As you begin to align your Core Values with your daily practices, you will begin to feel and become your more authentic self. Out of the core of your being, you will begin to see emerging out of her hiding place, the BREATHTAKING, WONDERFUL woman that you have been waiting to see. She is in there. She is waiting for you to give her permission to take her rightful place. When she is in charge, you will find that you are more confident, more effective and happier than you've ever been before.

Most of us have never taken the time to actually consider what we want our future to look like, much less what we need to do in order to attain our vision. I'm not necessarily talking about career goals, or education, or activity.

In this chapter, you will have two exercises: the first will help you define the kind of life you want and the second will give you a tool to help achieve that life.

Exercise #1

Imagery is a very powerful tool. Professional athletes are taught to imagine crossing the goal line or winning the race. Professional musicians are taught to imagine the performance. The Bible also tells us that 'whatsoever things we ask when we pray, believe that we have them and they shall be done for us.'

Let me explain.

Researchers in a 2013 Dartmouth College study determined that the brain has a "mental workspace" that consciously manipulates images, symbols, ideas and theories." Within this neural network the brain is able to have a laser-like focus to solve complex problems and come up with new ideas. [ii]

Take for instance, a common word like banana. Do you see the letters first or a yellow, tasty fruit?

The first exercise in "I Want", is to find a space of at least 45 minutes when you can be uninterrupted and alone.

Grab a notebook or piece of paper to be ready to write down your thoughts as soon as you have finished the exercise.

In this time, it is okay to have music playing SOFTLY in the background if it helps you to relax. Dim the lights, and give yourself permission to relax and dream.

Here are your instructions:

Imagine yourself on **THE PERFECT** day five or ten years from now. [iii]

Who are you with?

Where are you?

What is surrounding you?

What are the colors?

What are the fragrances?

What are you doing?

What are you wearing?

What are you listening to in the background?

Are you eating? What are you eating?

How are you feeling? Happy? Content? Excited?

You get the idea.

Consider that you are looking at a SNAPSHOT FORWARD instead of in the past. Observe EVERYTHING in the snapshot. This is the life you want to have if everything falls into line.

It may take a little bit of time to release yourself into the activity, but as you do simply allow your mind to create the scene for you. This is your mental workspace_creating the world as you would like to see it from all of the thoughts, feelings and dreams you've had over your lifetime. It is pulling together The images you've collected to paint a picture of your Ideal day. Enjoy it!

Before you re-engage with the world outside the door of your sanctuary, take a good amount of time to write down all that you saw and felt. Use as much detail as possible. Again, use either a notebook you may have grabbed for earlier exercises, or make notes in the back of this book.

How close are you to living that picture of your life? Do you have a bit of a journey ahead of you? That's okay. Are you pretty close? Fabulous!

This exercise is a tool you can go back to time and time again in your life in order to make sure that you are headed in the right direction.

What kind of emotions are you experiencing as you think about what you just envisioned? Are you happy or frustrated? Are you hopeful? Do you believe that life can be yours? What's holding you back? What's helping you move forward?

In the next section, we'll use a tool made popular by Steven Covey in The 7 Habits of Highly Effective People, called "Begin with the End in Mind." I call it "Thinking from the End."

Our goal with this exercise is to create a plan for the life we just envisioned. Today, all we're creating is a bare bones skeleton that will give us a launching pad.

I do suggest that for more complete instructions that you read the book by Steven Covey [iv]mentioned in the last chapter.

For me as a Christian, this concept is nothing new. The Bible tells us that God saw the end of all things before anything was created. He sees 'the end from the beginning.'

Exercise #2

I have found that the most effective way of 'doing' this process is to have a sheet of paper for each 'image' you'll be investigating.

It will make more sense as we go along.

For instance, say that you are creating a worksheet for is a personal life scene.

In that scene you probably saw certain people (or kinds of people), a certain environment, all involved in certain activities.

Let's use the following example:

A group of people are gathered on a covered patio. You can see the side of the Ranch Style home on the outskirts of the patio area. On the patio is a white wicker patio furniture set. Bright blue and green cushions are covering the chairs. Men and women of all ages are sitting around the glass patio table with brightly colored glasses in front of them. There are children running and playing in the yard and a puppy is chasing them. There is a Bar-B-Que grill with fragrant wood smoke wafting to the heavens. A person is standing by the grill calling over to the people on the patio. Someone is in the door to the house answering back. The sun is shining. The grass is green and perfectly manicured. The trees are lush; full of leaves and fruit. The garden areas are an explosion of bright yellow, orange and red and fragrance drifts through the air on the light breeze. A splash and laughter comes from the pool area. Birds are singing and music is playing in the background. Everyone is happy.

Can you see this? Can you hear it? Can you smell it? Maybe this is your everyday experience. I hope so (if it's what you want.) GO YOU!

For some people it might happen once in a while, for a few people rarely, and for many - never. But, the question is - if you want it - what does it take to GET it?

This is where 'Thinking from the End' comes into play and why the previous exercise is so important.

Here are the steps to use to create the vision you see for yourself.

Step 1 - Identify all of the aspects of the scene that are not your current reality; city, people, income required, property to purchase, etc.

Step 2 - What has to be in place for these things to be a reality? A move? A different job? Education? Marriage?

Step 3 - What are some activities that you can put into place RIGHT NOW that will move you in the direction you want to go?

Step 4 - What are some activities that you can put into place within the next 6 months to 1 year to move you in the direction you want to go?

Perhaps when you saw the original vision of what you want your life to be, it felt impossible. My hope is that if you will take the time to consider what it requires to have it come true, AND IF YOU ARE WILLING to put those requirements into action, you will see that it is NOT impossible. At the very least, you will have achieve a semblance of the life you desire.

The more precise you are with the details, the more tools you will create for yourself to attain your vision.

You may be thinking to yourself, "This is a very nice practice, but what does it have to do with me being wonderful or mentoring other women."

I've learned over the years that it only takes a little bit of control over your own life to feel less like a victim and more like a victor. When we lose the perception of ourselves that we will never, or can never, attain our goals and dreams, we become happier, more joyful, more focused and able to release the past that often has such a grip on us.

Take some encouragement from this:

Isaiah 61:1-3, 7 (New Living Translation of the Bible)

[1]The Spirit of the Sovereign Lord is upon me, for the Lord has anointed me to bring good new to the poor.

He has sent me to comfort the brokenhearted and to proclaim that captives will be released and prisoners will be freed.

2He has sent me to tell those who mourn that the time of the Lord's favor has come, and with it, the day of God's anger against their enemies.

3To all who mourn in Israel, He will give a crown of beauty for ashes, a joyous blessing instead of mourning, festive praise instead of despair. In their righteousness, they will be like great oaks that the Lord has planted for His own glory.

7Instead of shame and dishonor, you will enjoy a double share of honor. You will possess a double portion of prosperity in your land, and everlasting joy will be yours.

How we see ourselves dictates how we see the world around us and our place within it.

We've discussed the "I Am" of our life - the roles we fill and how we believe we perform within those roles.

We've looked at our Core Values and whether or not we are living our lives authentically.

We've touched on our Self Talk and ways to change our internal (sometimes external) language to and about ourselves.

And we've taken some time to dream and plan a bit about how we would like life to look sometime down the road.

For the last few moments of this section, I'd like for us to think about how you see yourself in the world.

I was watching a cooking program earlier this week and for their challenge they had to pick teams. The last player picked was what most would call a quirky, petite woman. The incredible thing to me is that in the weeks before she had proved herself to be a very good cook, albeit, even in her own terms, a little challenged at interpersonal relationships. In fact, one of her reasons to try out for the program was to help her be better at interacting with people.

It threw me back to childhood days and the common practice of 'choosing up sides.' Maybe I should interject here that I'm NOT of the opinion that 'everyone should be a winner and get a prize for participating.' Life just isn't that way and we shouldn't create a generation of people who think that it is. Perhaps though, you can relate to the story.

Oftentimes, we perceive ourselves by what order we were or are picked. And perhaps, the order in which we are picked is a reflection of how we see ourselves. I'm sure that they run into each other creating a never ending circle. That is until YOU or I decide that we don't like the picking (pecking?) ⱽorder.

If you see yourself as a #1 Draft Choice - then you tend to be more confident. If you don't, then anytime you go into an unfamiliar situation you will react with hesitation, which translates into nervousness.

Earlier, I spoke about being a happy, talking, laughing, spinning little girl. I felt loved and special and important when I twirled into a room. As I became unsure of life and my place in it, I became shy and withdrawn. I didn't feel like a precious, little girl anymore and thus, I began to hesitate when I walked into a room. I began to believe that my sister was loved more than me. It became harder and harder for me to interject myself into unfamiliar social situations and I felt more and more awkward the older I became. Even in the areas I excelled, it was hard for me to perform in front of others.

To compensate, I used what I had been taught and held my head up high. I thought I was already invisible so I might as well stand tall. To others, it translated as snobby. My personal perceptions were entirely different than what I portrayed.

There were areas and cliques I belonged to that had to do with the things I felt confident in - music being one. I had a lot of friends and some incredible experiences. However, true to form, I wanted to be with other groups. My confidence kept me out - not them. I didn't feel like I belonged, so I didn't.

As an adult woman, I've learned that oftentimes the quiet person in the corner is simply hoping for someone to include them. Sometimes the loudest person is the most afraid. Sometimes the most assured-seeming person is the most broken. Sometimes the prettiest girl is the most unsure. Sometimes the average-seeming person is the one who is most unique. As a leader of many different sizes and types of organizations, I've made it my goal to make sure EVERY person in the group has a place and opportunity to express themselves. Some excel in the front of the room, some within the structure. Some have never had an opportunity to lead and once given that chance, they become the most extraordinary leaders in the group.

Because I saw the world around me with the attitude of an outsider, I became a person who wanted others to feel included. Thankfully, I have been able to take something that could have crippled me and turned it into a way to reach out to the people around me.

I do continue to feel out of place sometimes. I believe everyone does. My tool to overcome? Go up to someone else who seems to feel out of place and say hello. Because I've learned, and continue to learn, that we all have treasures hidden inside of us, I want to be a person that helps others discover and release those treasures.

How you see yourself in this world depends on whether or not you see the broken areas in your life as opportunities to grow, or opportunities to hide away. A broken bone becomes stronger at the place it heals. A scar becomes a stronger area of skin. A wounded heart can, pardon the cliché', b e c o m e better - or bitter.

For your final exercise in this section, take a bit of time and think about how you see yourself in the world and how you fit within its framework. Are you happy with how things are? FABULOUS! Unhappy? How about taking what is stopping you and turning it into a tool to launch you forward into the life that You want. Don't know how? Hopefully, by the end of this book you'll decide to become a community member of our Women Mentoring Women group, W.O.R.K. (More about that at the end.)

Look Outward

Define what a MENTOR is and what a mentor does.

Mentors provide professional networks, outlets for frustration, college and career counseling, general life advice, and most importantly, an extra voice telling a student they are smart enough and capable enough to cross the stage at graduation and land their first paycheck from a career pathway job. Gerald Chertavian[vi]

Mentor or Coach, these both describe someone who assists you on your selected journey. You might decide to have one or more for both your personal and business needs.

A life or business coach is defined as a private teacher who gives lessons on a particular subject and will typically involve a formal arrangement. Your coaching experience may last only a short, prescribed amount of time.

A **mentor** is defined as a trusted advisor. It appears to come from two words meaning 'one who thinks or admonishes with intent, purpose, spirit and passion.' A mentor may be someone you know or desire to meet; someone who inspires you and influences your behavior.

Maya Angelou is quoted as saying, "In order to be a mentor, and an effective one, one must care. You must care. You don't have to know how many square miles are in Idaho, you don't need to know what is the chemical makeup of chemistry, or of blood or water. Know what you know and care about the person, care about what you know and care about the person you're sharing with. So if you know how to change a tire and that's all, that's good. But teach them by showing, by caring that they know these things."

It is obvious that a mentoring relationship is designed to propel you to not just perform a task in a better way, but to bring inspiration into your life. A mentor is someone who helps you discover not only the HOW of something, but also the WHY. A mentorship may be either a formal or informal arrangement. You may have people that have been mentors to you and that label was never placed on the relationship. Additionally, you may have been, or may be now, a mentor to someone. You may not even know that you are a mentor! The heart of mentorship is to help a person become a better version of herself.

Oprah Winfrey was mentored by her 4th grade teacher.

Dr. Phil McGraw was mentored by Oprah Winfrey.

Gloria Estefan was mentored by her grandmother.

Quincy Jones was mentored by Ray Charles.

Gwyneth Paltrow was mentored by Madonna.

Christian Dior was mentored by Yves St. Laurent.

Dr. Martin Luther King chose Mahatma Gandhi as his role model and was mentored by his life.

Only **YOU** limit what is possible. Now that you've used the earlier exercises and discovered what you want, find someone who's done it and follow them. Ask for their counsel, take what they've done and make it your own according to your authentic core values.

In the business world, women are less likely to have a mentor than men are! This has been cited by some experts as one of the reasons women do not ascend the business success ladder as quickly as men. Mentors differ from advisers in that they provide both psychosocial functions, such as role modeling, acceptance and affirmation, as well as career functions, such as sponsorship, coaching and networking, say the experts. [vii]

In our personal life, we used to be taught by our extended family of mothers, aunts and grandmothers on how to run and organize our home and family. So much of that mentorship has been left behind as our society has changed over the decades. Today, your mentor for how to be a good wife may be a woman at work or at church. Perhaps the person who helps you create systems to organize your home is someone you met at a Girl's Night Out. Regardless of the relationship, it simply comes down to the fact that we as women need to BE and GET mentors.

"God did not create you to be alone. He deposited skills, knowledge, and talents in someone out there who is expected to mentor you, teach you and encourage you to go high. Go, get a mentor!"

—Israelmore Ayivor, The Great Hand Book of Quotes

And to that I will say, someone is looking for YOU! Go, BE a mentor!

Look Around

Identify areas where you can use your gifts, callings, talents and core values to become a mentor.

Also, identify areas where you could use a mentor to assist you in reaching your life goals.

You are already a mentor, whether or not you know it. Someone is watching you and learning from you.

Someone is already YOUR mentor. You admire them and the way they live their life, so you are patterning certain things about yourself after their patterns.

Hopefully, after working through the exercises in the earlier chapters you've already discovered some of the strengths (and weaknesses) that make up your personality.

The next part of the discovery is looking at: 1) how to release the gifts you have, and 2) finding someone to help you grow in the areas you'd like to grow.

This is the thing, MENTORING is a big and sometimes scary word, but it is something all of us do. The important thing is to realize that there are things you are good at doing that would benefit someone else.

Mentoring others involves more than just the 'doing' of a task. Mentoring also involves the 'why' of a task. Additionally, there are special considerations of the environment itself that the mentoring addresses that will be brought into play.

Mentoring in a work environment involves helping someone know who to meet, what to do when they meet them, and how to present a positive, professional presence.

Mentoring in a home environment involves helping someone know how to do the tasks to create a smooth running home, and the benefits that are derived when it is has been created.

Mentoring in an informal environment could be anything from learning a skill set of how to be a Little League coach to holding a birthday party to organizing books on a shelf.

I Want to Teach...

If I am walking with two other men, each of them will serve as my teacher. I will pick out the good points of the one and imitate them, and the bad points of the other and correct them in myself.

--Confucius[viii]

Our first exercise will help you identify some of the things that you are good at doing.

List your technical skills (things you've received training for or that you've learned 'on-the-job')

1.

2.

3.

4.

5.

6.

7.

8.

9.

10.

Now, go back and highlight or put a * next to the things you believe you could teach someone else to do - even if you believe that you only know enough to teach them at a beginning level.

List the things that you like to do for recreation or in your quiet time.

1.

2.

3.

4.

5.

6.

7.

8.

9.

10.

Now, go back and highlight or put a * next to the things you believe you could teach someone else to do - even if you believe that you only know enough to teach them at a beginning level.

List the things that you do all the time, without even thinking about it, that could be considered a 'practical' skill. These are the things that are important to know how to do in everyday life - like washing dishes.

1.

2.

3.

4.

5.

6.

7.

8.

9.

10.

Now, go back and highlight or put a * next to the things you believe you could teach someone else to do - even if you believe that you only know enough to teach them at a beginning level.

There are most likely strengths that do not fall into any of the above categories; things like organizational skills, speaking to groups, and sewing or perhaps informal teaching skills you haven't received traditional training to do. List them below.

1.

2.

3.

4.

5.

6.

7.

8.

9.

10.

Now, go back and highlight or put a * next to the things you believe you could teach someone else to do - even if you believe that you only know enough to teach them at a beginning level.

Pick 2 items from each of the previous lists, that you enjoy the most and believe you could teach someone to accomplish. These are just a few of the things you could mentor someone else to accomplish! These more likely fall under the category of 'callings' because they are things that bring you joy. You were made for these!

1.

2.

3.

4.

5.

6.

7.

8.

Your next task is to begin to look around for places to share your gifts, talents and callings. Now that you have an idea of WHAT those are, you can begin to find WHO might could use your assistance in learning a new skill, breaking through life-long barriers, or simply how to make an incredible meal for her family.

I Want to Learn...

Take the attitude of a student, never be too big to ask questions, never know too much to learn something new.

-Og Mandino[ix]

Recognizing your WANT and NEED for a mentor requires a humble attitude and spirit. Without recognizing our need we'll never look for anyone to help us and once we've found someone to help, we have to have the attitude of a student; a learner; a receiver of knowledge.

Our Mentor might be younger than we. How are we going to respond to their teaching? Our Mentor might be someone that is of a different socio-economic class or background than we. How will we receive from them?

This is TRUTH…ALL of us have something to teach and ALL of us have something to learn.

The following exercises will help you identify some of the areas you would like to find a mentor.

<u>Workplace - I'd like to learn:</u>

1.

2.

3.

4.

5.

Home - I'd like to learn:

1.

2.

3.

4.

5.

Social Settings - I'd like to learn:

1.

2.

3.

4.

5.

There is an old proverb that says something like, 'When the student is ready, the teacher will appear." I believe that once we have identified the areas in which we want to grow that opportunities begin to open up before us.

Part of my heart's desire is that through this book and the W.O.R.K. community women from all over the U.S. and the world will begin to assist one another. My hope and prayer is that we will begin to create a mentoring network. YOU can be an integral part of this network.

As a person with skills and talents you can mentor someone else. As others join the community, your needs and desires for a mentor will be met as well.

Is it too bold to say that I can see W.O.R.K. chapters in the cities of America; women helping women and women teaching girls?

Look Forward

Creating Legacy by interacting with the next generation.

Here's something from a modern day poet, John Mayer and his song, "Daughters" – "Girls become lovers who turn into mothers. So mothers, be good to your daughters too."

I've thought quite a bit about my thoughts about my mom over the years. In the words I've written about her I'm hoping you haven't taken away the wrong view of her. I think she is one of the most extraordinary women I know. The life that she's lived and the history she's experienced boggle my mind. The life changes that occurred for her are experienced today only in developing countries, or someone who moves from a 'third-world' country to a modern: dirt floors, no electricity or running water, no indoor plumbing. Little food, little money, little hope for a different future. Our society as a whole changed, else she would have had the same existence that her mother had up until the late 40's & 50's. WWII created an entirely different world for women. With men gone, doors were of necessity opened up for women. Many of those doors closed again when the men came home, but the women were forever changed.

When I consider all my mother has experienced in her life – culturally, personally and generationally – I'm astounded. Life has completely changed for the women of her generation. And the pace that the world is changing is moving ever more quickly. Who knows what my granddaughter will have experienced by the time she's my age. She's grown up with internet technologies, game systems, Kindle tablet and cell phone as normal. I only began to work with a computer when I was in my late 20's and dial up internet was a luxury well into my 30's. Today, I'm sitting at a doctor's office with my husband, typing this into Windows Cloud on my iPad. My mother grew up with no phone, and as a little girl, our home phone was one phone attached to the wall with a dial and a long cord connecting the phone to the receiver so I could go around the corner. My granddaughter lives in a world of video chat and multiple cell phones in the household.

Let me say again, we are more connected than ever, yet seem to be less in relationship than any time in our history. It is almost impossible to have a conversation with someone without one or the other of the people looking at their cell phone. Meals are interrupted with phone calls and texts. We sit in rooms together with our headphones on and our faces glued to tablets, phones and games. Few families sit down together for meals anymore. Mom may go out once in a while with her friends for a "Wine and Canvas" evening, but time with her daughter is probably to and from softball, track or some school function. Conversation about what it is to be a woman in today's world may have bold language, but most young girls are learning more from their peers and the media than their moms. I'm
not coming down on moms either. It's just the way the world is today. With the media images thrown at

Girls through commercials during cartoons, it's hard for a parent to be able to control the images a girl will see and how she will interpret them. Even the best parenting plan has to navigate the mine field of social media, the press, TV and movies. Girls play with dolls called 'Bratz' and their role models are celebrities that are in the news more for their meltdowns than their great achievements. Models for adult fashion are 14 and made to look as if they are 20, and 20 year old fashion models are afraid they are too old to be relevant. Childhood innocence is a thing of the past.

How in this world, do we create a legacy of right attitudes for our daughters and granddaughters?

I know that there are great organizations out there, doing incredible work, to help change laws so our girls will be protected. However, the real work has to be done on an almost 'cellular' level. That is, when we think about the WHOLE BODY of womanhood who is struggling, the work to change things for the future must include a powerful strategy for mentoring and assisting young girls at a very early age.

I certainly don't have all the answers for this HUGE need, but what I know is that there are women who do have the answers, who would love an opportunity to work with other women with the same passion for change.

My hope is that we will work together to create an environment of dialogue and help for the young women following after us.

Resource Organizations

Below I'm going to list some of the more well-publicized organizations. The information included with each organization comes directly from their websites. I'm not endorsing them, they are simply a starting place for your search to know how you might become involved in a bigger way.

GEMS – Girls Educational and Mentoring Services, assisting girls who are victims of sexual abuse and sex trafficking.

Divine Images Network, Inc. - an organization that is committed to promoting economic and social empowerment of women and girls, so they can be of greater service to their communities, our nation and one another.

Sisters of Hope - an organization that provides empowerment programs targeting women and girls. Sisters of Hope is one of the leading Women & Girls Empowerment organizations in the U.S. offering various events and programs that encourage girls to express themselves artistically through visual and performing arts.

Girls Today Women Tomorrow - empowers girls to create their own opportunities for life success through contributing to their community as young leaders guided by mentors dedicated to expanding their horizons.

Million Women Mentors - is a ground-breaking collaborative effort designed to engage one million science, technology, engineering and math (STEM) mentors. The initiative aims to educate and empower girls and young women to actively pursue STEM education and careers.

Boys and Girls Clubs of America - Club programs and services promote and enhance the development of boys and girls by instilling a sense of competence, usefulness, belonging and influence.

If you know of a group or organization that is doing great work, will you let me know? I'd love to list them on the resources page of my website.

W.O.R.K. is NOT a 4-Letter Word

I had a dream when I was in my twenties. I could see women of all ages, all backgrounds, and all education levels who had joined together to support one another. Women with experience and expertise assisted those who were learning. Women with needs were made to feel strong and supported by the others. *(And in some way, aren't we all 'needy?')* Every woman had something to contribute to the good of the others.

The name of the organization may sound a bit odd; **W.O.R.K.** which stands for *Women of the Royal Kingdom*.

The dictionary definition of **WORK** is: *1) activity involving mental or physical effort done in order to achieve a purpose or result.*

I am creating a group of women to carry out the mandate that I received as that very young woman. Women who will **WORK** with me in order to achieve the result of creating a network of BREATHTAKING, loving, supportive, and mindful women to assist one another along our journey. You see, I know one thing for certain: you're never too old to pursue the things that are in your heart. There is a time for everything, and this is that time.

Psalm 45:10-17 has become a foundational scripture to me in this endeavor.

10 Listen to me, O royal daughter, take to heart what I say. Forget your people and your family far away.
(My thought: forget the past and the negative things that have been said about you – by yourself and others.)

11 For your royal husband delights in your beauty; honor him, for he is your lord.

12The princess of Tyre will shower you with gifts. The wealthy will beg your favor.

13 The bride, a princess, looks glorious in her golden down.

14 In her beautiful robes, she is led to the king accompanied by her bridesmaids.

15 What a joyful and enthusiastic procession as they enter the king's palace!

16 Your sons will become kings like their father. You will make them rulers over many lands.

17 I will bring honor to your name in every generation. Therefore, the nations will praise you forever and ever.

Dr. John C. Maxwell describes four kinds of people in his article, "Whatever It Takes." [x]These four types of people are:

Cop-outs - set no goals and make no decisions

Hold-outs - have beautiful dreams but are afraid to respond to the challenges because they lack the self-confidence to overcome the difficulties

Drop-outs - clearly define their goals, and in the beginning, work hard to make their dreams come true. But when the going gets tough, they quit.

All-outs - These are the stars that want to shine out as an inspiration to others. Once they've set their goals, they never quit - no matter the price and challenges. They have a can-do attitude that carries them to their greatness.

So, will you join me as we empower and encourage women to remember their greatness? Will you find your place in the **All-Outs?** You see, your circle of influence is vast. Together we can reach to the corners of the earth. You probably already know women who are working in this realm. I know I do. Gathering together all of the different forces that are around us we can make changes. The changes that occur will be from within, and those are after all, the most powerful changes that can happen.

What Next?

The ability to believe in your own greatness will greatly determine whether or not you move forward. Often, even when we want to believe something is truth, we can get stuck in old patterns of thinking. We can't seem to make the step from knowing the truth, into believing the truth. And if you can't believe it, you can't live it.

This is when a little help can empower us to make that critical step. In my life, this has been the place where a coach has made the difference.

A coach is not necessarily a psychologist, a doctor, nor a licensed therapist. A coach is someone who walks with you through a process to develop skills and confidence. A coach reminds me of Glinda the Good Witch of the Wizard of Oz. She tells Dorothy, "My dear, you had the power to go home within you all along."

A good coach will not tell you WHAT to do, but will help you to recognize and draw out the power that is within you to make the changes you desire.

There are many types of coaches; from life, to business development, to health or executive leadership. Depending on the changes you want to see implemented in your life, you have your choice of a never-ending supply of people whose one aim is to help you achieve your goals.

A coach is invested in your success, and has compassion on your situations, but doesn't become co-dependent with you in the circumstances. In other words, your coach holds you accountable for the decisions and actions you make, or don't make.

Not only have I had the benefit of having a coach, I have the privilege of being a coach. I've worked with women of all ages and backgrounds navigate both life issues, and business building strategies.

I'd like to offer you the opportunity to have a free thirty minute coaching session with me. During that time, we can discuss some of the areas you might feel a bit stuck. After the complimentary session, we can discuss whether you believe you could benefit from continuing in a paid coaching relationship with me.

Along with my elite program of private, one-on-one coaching, I offer focused group coaching, which includes partnering with others on the same goal path; group coaching for your organization to address relationship or business building skills; and, regular teleseminars and webinars.

Additionally, I am available to speak and train to groups, large and small, on subjects that pertain to women and their lives and business.

No matter which of these will benefit you, know that I am committed to working with you to help bring YOUR goals to life. You have a God-ordained destiny. I would be honored to be His vessel to walk beside you on the road to the realization of your dreams and visions.

You can learn more about available programs at http://donnawoolam.com/coaching.

#####

JOIN ME!

Share Your Story!

Will you consider sharing your transformational journey with me and the other women out there who are just like us? We all need an inspiration to help us continue the journey. Your story may be the one that helps another woman take one more step.

In an upcoming volume of *Breathtaking Stories of Women* your story could be featured as a model for someone else. You can indicate your desire to share your story by going to my website http:// donnawoolam.com and filling out the contact information form. Just let me know that you have a story to tell. Perhaps you know someone who has inspired you. We'd love to hear her story, too!

How to Get Involved in W.O.R.K.

If you are interested in becoming a member of the W.O.R.K. organization, please take a minute to go to my website http://donnawoolam.com and let me know that you are interested in becoming involved in the W.O.R.K. movement. This organization is in its infancy. If you are a woman who believes in building up other women, you are welcome.

Add Your Review and Comments!

If this book has been an inspiration to you will you do me another favor or two?

Please take just a minute to go to your favorite online book site and give a review and rating for this book. By doing so, your evaluation could draw more women to read this book and be encouraged, as well as empowered.

Once you've written the review, please share the book store link to your Social Media sites and encourage your friends to download their own copy of the book.

If you have a comment or suggestion to make a change or correction to this book, please EMAIL those to me from my website.

One Last Thing...

A huge thank you goes out to two special women. I was admonished to have people who would be brutally honest look over the drafts of this book. They had to be people I trusted, who cared about me. Carol Watson and Monique Waggoner are those women. I love them for their honesty, clarity and insight as to what this manuscript needed. You have made me better and I love you for it.

About Donna K Woolam

I was raised in the Panhandle of Texas in Amarillo. I've spent most of my life in Texas with a stint just over a year in South Carolina where our youngest son Monty was born. Richard and I have been married for just over 36 wonderful years. I believe that the husband is the head of the household, and the wife is his partner. It doesn't make me 'less-than.' In fact, he treats me like a queen and loves me beyond what my heart can hold.

We raised two amazing sons, Dustin and Monty, whom are great men. They are a continual source of blessing and joy to me. I believe that children are a gift, a treasure, and that they do not make the decisions in the family.

I am Mother-in-law to one of the most captivating, smart and wise women I know, Jayme. Dustin and Jayme have made me grandmother to two amazing children - Calista and Ian. They give me joy that I never knew I could experience!

I've lived a life painted with many strokes of color and influence. I've worked from home as well as within the corporate structure. Our boys attended public school until the Dustin was in the 9th grade and Monty in the 7th and then I home-schooled them through graduation. While working away from home, I also attended Bible School at Knowing Him Bible Institute (alongside Richard) in order to become a minister of the Gospel and to share the Good News of Jesus Christ with others. We were pastors of a small congregation in West Texas for a time and we've worked in many other churches. I believe that the Word of God holds the final truth on any subject. I am a continual learner and don't think I know everything. I want to continue learning until the day I die. I am a writer, living out my dreams every day. I'm still wearing some of the garments my mother gave me, but now I wear them thankfully and joyfully.

Let's Be Friends!

Connect With Me

Other Books Available At:
http://livingatmybest.com

Friend me on Facebook:
http://facebook.com/TheLifeInspired

Follow me on Twitter:
http://twitter.com/donnakwoolam

Connect on LinkedIn:
http://linkedin.com/in/donnawoolam

Join My Online Community:
http://donnawoolam.com

Need a Speaker?

Please contact me through my website or email me at donna@donnawoolam.com.

Endnotes and References

[i] http://jennyhoople.com/blog/how-to-find-your-core-values

[ii] Dartmouth College. "How and where imagination occurs in human brains." ScienceDaily. ScienceDaily, 16 September 2013. <www.sciencedaily.com/releases/2013/09/130916162003.htm>.

[iii] From a mental exercise I learned from Steven Q Wiltshire, LifeLine Coaching.

[iv] Stephen R. Covey's book, *The 7 Habits of Highly Effective People*®, has been a top-seller for the simple reason that it ignores trends and pop psychology for proven principles of fairness, integrity, honesty, and human dignity; it is celebrating its fifteenth year of helping people solve personal and professional problems.

[v] From a Wikipedia Article on Pecking Order:

The ultimate function of a pecking order is to increase the individual or inclusive fitness of the animals involved in its formation. Fighting to acquire resources such as food and mates is expensive in terms of time, energy and the risk of injury. By developing a pecking order, animals determine which individuals will get priority of access to resources, particularly when they are limited; there is a reduction in aggression when a pecking order has been developed. Therefore, the proximate functions of a pecking order are to reduce the costs of time, energy and risk of injury incurred during resource acquisition and defence.

The basic concept behind the establishment of the pecking order among, for example, chickens, is that it is necessary to determine who is the 'top chicken,' the 'bottom chicken' and where all the rest fit in between. The establishment of the dominance hierarchy may reduce the incidence of conflict and thus reduce the expenditure of energy required for aggressive competition. The dominance level determines which individual gets preferential access to resources such as food and mates.[4]

In the wild, pecking order status is inherited along a strict basis, so that the first daughter of the most dominant chicken will inherit that most dominant status, the second most dominant will give second most dominant status to her daughter, etc. unless the most dominant chicken has a second daughter, in which case that chicken will become the second most dominant.[citation needed] Studies of the genetic basis of pecking orders in chickens have indicated that it may largely be determined by the coloration patterns.[5]

It is not necessary for animals to be able to recognise individuals within the group for a pecking order to be maintained. Animal behaviours may be motivated by "rule of thumb". For example, if chickens can predict the fighting ability of others simply by assessing their body size, they will be able to maintain the hierarchy whilst avoiding a fight which could cause injury and will be energetically costly. Using this rule of thumb, if Chicken A sees that Chicken B is larger, Chicken A will defer; if Chicken B is smaller, it will defer to Chicken A. In this way, only chickens of similar sizes will fight and the pecking order of the group overall is maintained without requiring individual recognition.

Wild and feral chickens form relatively small groups, usually including no more than 10 to 20 individuals. It has been shown that in larger groups, which is common in farming, the dominance hierarchy becomes less stable and aggression increases.[6]

[vi] Read more at http://www.brainyquote.com/quotes/quotes/g/geraldcher6 16035.html#34WcvKBCpDqxVzfD.99

[vii] American Psychological Association

By MARGARET SCHLEGEL; November 2000, Vol 31, No. 10; Print version: page 33

[viii] Read more at
http://www.brainyquote.com/quotes/quotes/c/confucius11
8477.html#Bj12oTTxuxvS1xYv.99

[ix] Read more at:
htttp://www.brainyquote.com/quotes/quotes/o/ogmandino
134856.html#Qb2o8CxhAMFp61Id.99

[x] Whatever It Takes—The Keys to Unlocking a Can-Do Attitude By Dr. John C. Maxwell